Butterflies and moths are insects.
They all have wings and six legs.

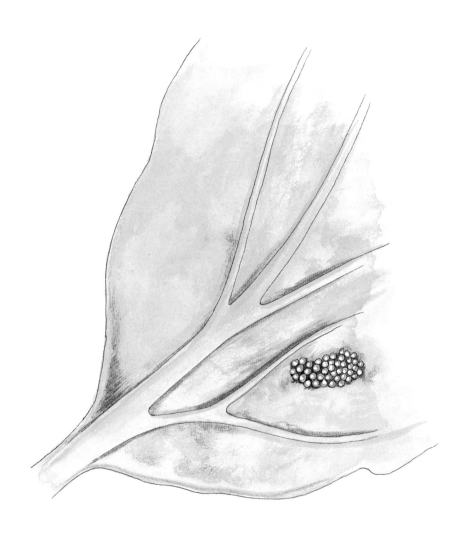

Butterflies and moths start as eggs.

Caterpillars hatch from the eggs. They munch and munch and get bigger and bigger.

As the caterpillar gets bigger, its skin splits, but it keeps on feeding and getting bigger.

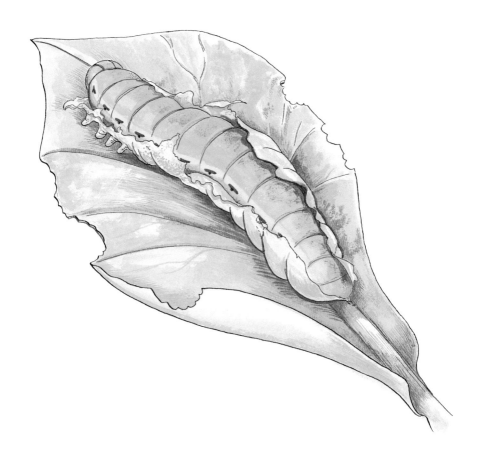

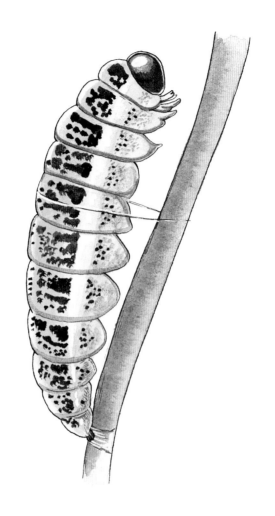

Then the caterpillar attaches itself to a stem or a twig, and spins a silk skin around itself.

This skin forms a hard shell, which splits to let the insect out.

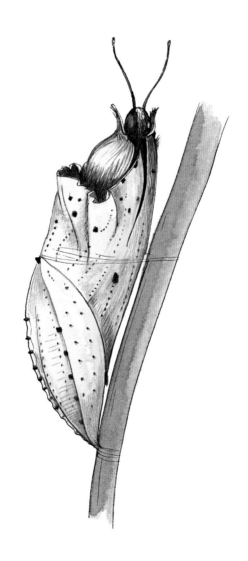

Butterflies and moths have
a mouth called a proboscis.
They suck up nectar with it.

Butterflies' feelers have knobs on the end. Moths' feelers do not, and often look fluffy.

Some moths, but not all of them, come out in the dark. There are more different sorts of moths than there are different sorts of butterflies.

A lot of butterflies die when winter comes. In the spring, butterflies start to hatch again.

Some butterflies and moths have tails. The comet moth has a long tail.

An atlas moth can be
as big as a magpie!